If you are looking for easy and fast recipes to cook with your kids, then this dessert recipes book is the perfect choice! It features easy and tasty chicken recipes that are easy to prepare and cook. Not only will your kids enjoy cooking these recipes, but they will also learn how to prepare them in a fun way. The recipes are easy to follow, with easy-to-understand instructions that any child or beginner cook can understand. Whether you're looking for something savory and delicious or something sweet and light, this book has it all! With its wide variety of easy desserts perfect for the whole family, this is a must-have in every kitchen.

Chocolate Brownie Cake

Ingredients
100g butter
125g caster sugar
75g light brown or muscovado sugar
125g plain chocolate (plain or milk)
1 tbsp golden syrup
2 eggs
1 tsp vanilla extract/essence
100g plain flour
½ tsp baking powder
2 tbsp cocoa powder

If you're looking for a simple yet delicious kid-friendly dessert recipe, a chocolate brownie cake is the perfect choice. Not only does it look and taste amazing, but it's easy to make too! All you need are some basic ingredients such as butter, caster sugar, light brown or muscovado sugar, plain chocolate of your choice (plain or milk), golden syrup, eggs, vanilla extract/essence, plain flour, baking powder and cocoa powder. Simply mix all the ingredients together in a bowl until well combined. You can even get your little ones involved to help make this delightful treat for the whole family! Once baked, you'll have yourself a delicious chocolate brownie cake that everyone will enjoy! Kid-friendly desserts have never been so easy and delicious. Try out this chocolate brownie cake recipe today for a fun, sweet treat!

Vanilla Cupcakes

Ingredients
110g butter, softened
110g golden caster sugar
2 eggs
1 tsp vanilla extract
110g self-raising flour
1-2 tbsp milk, plus a little extra for the icing
For the icing
125g butter, softened
185g icing sugar

Vanilla Cupcakes are a great kid-friendly dessert recipe! They're easy to make, and you only need a few simple ingredients. To get started, preheat your oven to 180°C/Gas Mark 4. In a large bowl, cream together the butter and golden caster sugar until light and fluffy. Beat in the eggs one at a time, then stir in the vanilla extract. Sift in the self-raising flour, then add 1-2 tablespoons of milk and mix until just combined.

Line a 12-cupcake tin with cupcake cases and divide the mixture between them – they should be about two thirds full. Bake for 15–20 minutes, or until a skewer inserted into the centre of a cupcake comes out clean. Transfer to a wire rack to cool completely.

For the icing, cream together the softened butter and icing sugar until light and fluffy. If it's too thick, add a little extra milk. Once the cupcakes are cooled, top each one with a generous dollop of the icing. Sprinkle with decorations of your choice, and you're done! Enjoy your delicious Kid Dessert Recipe - Vanilla Cupcakes!

Pancakes

This healthy breakfast recipe for kids is sure to become a family favorite! With only a few ingredients, it's easy to make and perfect for busy mornings. Start by mixing together 2 cups all-purpose flour, 2 teaspoons baking powder, ¼ teaspoon salt, and 1 tablespoon sugar (optional). Then add in the eggs and 1½ to 2 cups milk, and stir until the batter is smooth. Finally, add in 2 tablespoons melted and cooled butter (optional), or use a neutral oil for cooking. Heat up a skillet over medium-high heat and add butter or oil to coat the bottom of the pan. Drop about ¼ cup pancake batter into the pan per pancake. Cook until the edges begin to look golden and bubbles appear on the top of each pancake. Flip the pancakes over, cook for another minute or two, then remove from heat and serve with your favorite toppings! Enjoy! This healthy breakfast recipe for kids is not only easy to make but also incredibly delicious. Kids will love the fluffy pancakes and parents will love the healthy ingredients. The best part is that everyone can have breakfast ready in no time! With this healthy breakfast recipe for kids, you've got a surefire way to start your mornings off right. Enjoy!

Peanut Butter and Jelly Muffins

INGREDIENTS :
1 c. wheat bran
1 c. whole-wheat flour
1/2 c. granulated sugar
1 tsp. baking powder
1/2 tsp. baking soda
1/2 tsp. ground cinnamon
1 pinch kosher salt
1/4 c. unsweetened applesauce
1/2 c. buttermilk
1/4 c. olive oil
1 large egg
1 c. small red grapes
10 tsp. creamy peanut butter
1 tbsp. water
1/4 c. seedless jam

Are you looking for healthy recipes to make with your kids? Look no further than these delicious peanut butter and jelly muffins! Not only are they easy to make, but they're also a healthy alternative to traditional sugary desserts.

These muffins have an array of healthy ingredients such as wheat bran, whole-wheat flour, applesauce, buttermilk and olive oil. They also include a healthy dose of cinnamon and some delicious 10 teaspoons of creamy peanut butter!

To complete the recipe, you'll need to mix together 1 cup of small red grapes with 1 tablespoon of water and ¼ cup seedless jam. This mixture will be swirled throughout the muffin batter to create a delightful jammy surprise.

When all the ingredients are combined and baked, they make healthy and delicious muffins that your kids will love. Enjoy!

Hope you have fun making these healthy peanut butter and jelly muffins with your kids! They're sure to enjoy them as much as you do.

Happy baking!

Fruit Tart

Ingredients
220g plain flour, plus extra for dusting
1 tbsp golden caster sugar
110g unsalted butter, chilled and diced
1 large egg yolk
120g mascarpone
250ml double cream
1 tsp vanilla bean paste
1 tbsp icing sugar
300g fruit (we used cherries, redcurrants and various berries), chopped if necessary

This fruity tart is a delicious and simple way to get the kids involved in baking. With just a few ingredients, you can have this classic dessert served up in no time!
To make this Kid Dessert Recipe, you will need 220g plain flour plus extra for dusting, 1 tablespoon of golden caster sugar, 110g of unsalted butter chilled and diced, 1 large egg yolk, 120g of mascarpone, 250ml double cream, 1 teaspoon of vanilla bean paste, 1 tablespoon of icing sugar and 300g fruits (we used cherries, redcurrants and various berries) chopped if necessary.

First start by preheating the oven to 350 degrees F (175 degrees C). Then in a large bowl, add the plain flour and caster sugar and mix together. Add in the cold butter cubes, rubbing them into the flour mixture with your fingertips until it forms a breadcrumb like texture.

Next add in the egg yolk and 1 tablespoon of cold water. Mix together until it forms a soft dough. Then roll out the dough on a lightly floured surface and use it to line the base and sides of a 9-inch (23 cm) tart tin. Prick the base all over with a fork, then bake in preheated oven for 15 minutes until golden brown.

Once the pastry has cooked, remove it from the oven and allow to cool. In a separate bowl, add the mascarpone cheese, double cream and vanilla bean paste and whisk together until smooth. Spread this mixture over the cooled pastry base then top with your chosen fruits.

Finally sprinkle with icing sugar and serve! Enjoy

Easy Chocolate Cake

Ingredients
150ml sunflower oil, plus extra for the tin
175g self-raising flour
2 tbsp cocoa powder
1 tsp bicarbonate of soda
150g caster sugar
2 tbsp golden syrup
2 large eggs, lightly beaten
150ml semi-skimmed milk
For the icing
100g unsalted butter
225g icing sugar
40g cocoa powder
2½ tbsp milk (a little more if needed)

To make this easy chocolate cake you will need 150ml sunflower oil plus extra for the tin, 175g self-raising flour, 2 tablespoons cocoa powder, 1 teaspoon bicarbonate of soda, 150g caster sugar, 2 tablespoons golden syrup, 2 large eggs lightly beaten and 150ml semi-skimmed milk.

Preheat your oven to 180°C (gas mark 4). Grease and line a 20cm springform cake tin with baking parchment.

In a large bowl, sift together the flour, cocoa powder and bicarbonate of soda. Add in the caster sugar and mix until combined. In another bowl, whisk together the oil, golden syrup, beaten eggs and milk until fully blended.

Pour the wet ingredients into the dry ingredients and stir until everything is evenly combined. Then pour the mixture into your prepared cake tin and bake in the oven for 30 minutes or until a skewer inserted into the centre comes out clean.

Once your chocolate cake has cooled, it's time to make the icing! Beat together 100g of unsalted butter, 225g of icing sugar and 40g of cocoa powder in a bowl. Once combined, add 2½ tablespoons of milk and beat until light and fluffy. Spread over the top of your cake before serving. Enjoy!

Chocolate Chip Muffins

Chocolate chip muffins are a classic and Kid Friendly Dessert Recipe. Making them at home is fun, easy, and you can even get the kids to help out! All you need is 250g self-raising flour, 1 tsp bicarbonate of soda, 150g chocolate chips (milk, white, dark or a mix of all three), 100g golden caster sugar, 2 eggs, lightly beaten, 150ml natural yogurt and 100g unsalted butter, melted.

Start by preheating your oven to 180 degrees Celsius (160 fan). In a bowl, mix together the flour and bicarbonate of soda. Add in the chocolate chips and stir until evenly distributed. In a separate bowl, beat together the sugar, eggs and yogurt until smooth. Gradually add in the melted butter, mixing well to combine. Gently fold in the dry ingredients into the wet mixture until just combined.

Using an ice cream scoop or spoon, divide the muffin batter between cases placed on a baking tray. Bake for 20 minutes, or until golden and a skewer comes out clean when inserted. Allow to cool on the tray for 5 minutes before transferring to a wire rack.
Happy baking!

Buttermilk Pancakes

Ingredients
2 c. all-purpose flour
2 1/2 tbsp. granulated sugar
1 tsp. baking powder
1 tsp. baking osda
1 tsp. kosher salt
2 1/2 c. buttermilk
2 eggs, separated
4 tbsp. unsalted butter, melted, plus more for serving
Vegetable oil, for cooking
Maple syrup, for serving

These healthy buttermilk pancakes are the perfect choice for a delicious, nutritious breakfast. Not only are they full of healthy ingredients like all-purpose flour, granulated sugar, baking powder and baking soda, kosher salt, buttermilk, eggs, butter, and vegetable oil - they're also incredibly simple to make. With only a few steps and limited ingredients, kids can easily help make this healthy recipe.

To begin, whisk together the all-purpose flour, sugar, baking powder, baking soda and salt in a large bowl. In a separate bowl, whisk together the buttermilk and egg yolks until combined. Make sure to save the whites for later! Pour the buttermilk mixture into the flour mixture and stir until combined. Then add in the melted butter and mix until everything is smooth.

In a separate bowl, beat the egg whites with a hand mixer or whisk until stiff peaks form. Gently fold them into the batter using a spatula. Heat a large skillet over medium heat and brush with vegetable oil.

Using a 1/4 cup measuring cup, scoop the batter into the skillet and cook until golden brown on both sides. Serve with extra butter, maple syrup, or your favorite topping. This healthy recipe for kids is sure to be a hit! Enjoy!

Strawberry Muffins

Ingredients

½ cup milk
¼ cup canola oil
1 large egg
1 ¾ cups all-purpose flour
½ cup white sugar
2 teaspoons baking powder
½ teaspoon salt
1 cup chopped strawberries

Strawberry Muffins are a great healthy breakfast for kids. Not only are they delicious, but they're also easy to make using simple ingredients. All you need is milk, canola oil, an egg, all-purpose flour, sugar, baking powder and salt. Once you have these basic ingredients, the rest is just about adding your favorite fruits, like strawberries. Simply chop the strawberries and mix them into the batter for a tasty treat that your kids will love. Serve up these muffins with a glass of cold milk or juice and you've got a delicious breakfast! Healthy, easy and delicious - what more could you ask for? Your kids are sure to love these Strawberry Muffins.
Enjoy!

Pumpkin Oatmeal Cookies

Ingredients   2 Cup(s) flour, all-purpose
1 1/3 Cup(s) Quaker® Oats (quick or old fashioned)
1 Teaspoon(s) Baking Soda
1 Teaspoon(s) Cinnamon
1/2 Teaspoon(s) Salt
1 Cup(s) butter or margarine, softened
1 Cup(s) Sugar
1 Cup(s) Brown sugar, packed
1 Cup(s) canned pumpkin {NOT pumpkin pie filling}
1 Teaspoon(s) vanilla
3/4 Cup(s) Chopped Walnuts
3/4 Cup(s) raisins
1 Egg(s)

These delicious Pumpkin Oatmeal Cookies are the perfect way to give your kids a healthy start to their day. Packed full of nutritious ingredients like all-purpose flour, Quaker® Oats, baking soda, cinnamon, salt, butter or margarine, sugar, brown sugar, canned pumpkin (not pumpkin pie filling), vanilla extract, chopped walnuts, raisins, and one egg, these treats will provide a boost of energy to kick off their day. Plus, they're sure to love the sweet pumpkin flavor! Enjoy a warm batch of these cookies for breakfast and feel good about giving your kids a healthy start.
Enjoy!

Coconut Yoghurt Cake

INGREDIENTS

200g unsalted butter, at room temperature, chopped
2 tsp finely grated lime zest, plus extra to serve
3/4 cup (165g) caster sugar
3 eggs, at room temperature
60g fine semolina
1/2 cup (50g) almond meal
1 1/2 cups (225g) self-raising flour, sifted
3/4 cup (45g) shredded coconut
180g natural yoghurt
120ml lime juice
Whipped cream, to serve

SYRUP

370g caster sugar
Finely grated zest of 2 limes plus 1 cup (250ml) lime juice

Coconut Yoghurt Cake is a delicious dessert that you can make at home for any occasion. This cake requires just 200g of unsalted butter, 2 teaspoons of finely grated lime zest, 3/4 cup of caster sugar, 3 eggs, 60g of fine semolina, 1/2 cup of almond meal, 1 1/2 cups of self-raising flour, 3/4 cup of shredded coconut, 180g of natural yoghurt, 120ml lime juice and some whipped cream to serve.

To complete this dessert, you have to make a syrup. For the syrup, you will need 370g caster sugar and finely grated zest from 2 limes and 1 cup of lime juice. Once all the ingredients have been put together, you can bake the cake in a preheated oven of 160°C (320-325°F).

Once it's done baking, you can pour over the syrup and garnish with extra lime zest. Serve with whipped cream for a dessert that will impress your family and friends. If you are looking for easy dessert ideas to make at home, Coconut Yoghurt Cake is a great choice. Enjoy!

Ricotta Cake

INGREDIENTS

200g unsalted butter, chilled, chopped
1 3/4 cup (385g) caster sugar
5 eggs
3 cups (450g) plain flour
1 tsp baking powder
700g fresh ricotta
500g cream cheese, at room temperature
2 tsp vanilla extract
Pure icing sugar, to dust

Ricotta cake is a delicious dessert that can be easily prepared at home. It's one of those dessert ideas you can make without much fuss and it tastes great! The dessert starts with the basic ingredients: unsalted butter, caster sugar, eggs, plain flour, baking powder, fresh ricotta, cream cheese and vanilla extract. All these ingredients are combined to make a soft, light and creamy cake.

To prepare the dessert, first preheat the oven to 180C/160C fan-forced. Grease a 20cm round springform tin and line with baking paper. Beat butter and sugar in a bowl until light and creamy then add eggs one at a time, beating after each addition. Add sifted flour and baking powder and stir until just combined.

Spread half of the mixture into the prepared tin. In a separate bowl mix together ricotta, cream cheese and vanilla extract then spread over base in the tin. Top with remaining cake mixture and smooth top evenly. Bake for 1 hour or until a skewer inserted into the cake comes out clean.

Let the dessert sit in tin for 10 minutes before transferring to a wire rack to cool completely. When you're ready to serve, dust the top of the ricotta cake with pure icing sugar. Enjoy your dessert!

Sticky Ginger Pudding

INGREDIENTS
1 3/4 cups (260g) self-raising flour
1 1/2 tsp ground ginger
1/4 tsp bicarbonate of soda
100g dark muscovado sugar
2 tbs treacle
120g unsalted butter, chopped, melted
1/2 cup (125ml) buttermilk
3 eggs
150g uncrystallised ginger, finely chopped
Thickened cream or ice cream, to serve
GINGER SAUCE
100g unsalted butter, chopped
1/3 cup (75g) dark muscovado sugar
1/3 cup (80ml) ginger beer
200ml thickened cream
120g uncrystallised ginger, chopped

If you're looking for a dessert that's the perfect balance of sweet, sticky and spicy, look no further than Sticky Ginger Pudding. This classic dessert is easy to make at home with just a few ingredients. You'll need self-raising flour, ground ginger, bicarbonate of soda, dark muscovado sugar, treacle, unsalted butter, buttermilk, eggs and uncrystallised ginger. To make the dessert even more indulgent, it's served with a creamy Ginger Sauce made from chopped unsalted butter, dark muscovado sugar, ginger beer and thickened cream. Once you've prepared all the ingredients and put them together in a baking dish, pop it in the oven for about an hour. When it comes out, you'll be rewarded with a warm and comforting dessert that's sure to impress. Enjoy this classic dessert with friends and family for a truly delicious dessert experience.

Adding Sticky Ginger Pudding to your repertoire of dessert ideas is a great way to add a new twist to dessert night. With its delicious balance of sweetness, spice and stickiness, this comforting dessert is sure to be a hit with everyone. And thanks to its few simple ingredients, it's an easy dessert that you can make at home in no time. So why not give this tasty classic dessert a try? It's sure to become a dessert night favourite!

Enjoy!

Lime Pie Mousse

Ingredients

FOR THE CRUMBLE
4 graham crackers
3/4 c. rolled oats
1/3 c. packed light brown sugar
3 tbsp. all-purpose flour
6 tbsp. cold butter, cubed

FOR THE MOUSSE
1 1/2 c. heavy cream
1/4 c. powdered sugar
1 c. sweetened condensed milk
1/3 c. freshly squeezed key lime juice
1 tsp. pure vanilla extract
Green food coloring (optional)
Key lime wedges, for garnish

If you're looking for a dessert that is both delicious and easy to make at home, look no further than Lime Pie Mousse! This dessert combines the tartness of key lime juice with the sweetness of condensed milk and powdered sugar, all encased in a graham cracker crumble. It can be made in just a few simple steps with just a few ingredients, and the result is a dessert that is sure to please.

To make the crumble base of the mousse, you'll need graham crackers, rolled oats, light brown sugar, all-purpose flour, and cold butter. Start by crushing the graham crackers into small pieces and combining them with the other dry ingredients in a bowl. Add the cubed butter and mix until everything is well combined. Spread the mixture into an even layer on a greased baking sheet, and bake for about 15 minutes at 350 degrees Fahrenheit.

Once the crumble has cooled, it's time to make the mousse itself! Start by whipping together heavy cream and powdered sugar in a bowl until stiff peaks form. Then, add the sweetened condensed milk, key lime juice, and vanilla extract to the cream mixture, stirring until everything is well combined. If you want to give your dessert an extra pop of color, you can also add a few drops of green food coloring for effect.

Pour the mousse over the graham cracker crumble and spread it into an even layer. Refrigerate for at least 2 hours to allow the flavors to meld together. Serve with a few key lime wedges as a garnish, and enjoy! Your guests will be impressed by your dessert-making prowess when you serve up this delicious Lime Pie Mousse.
Give it a try and see for yourself!

Chocolate Pots De Crème

Ingredients
2 c. heavy cream
3 egg yolks
3 tbsp. granulated white sugar
Pinch kosher salt
1 tsp. pure vanilla extract
6 oz. bittersweet chocolate, chopped or broken into pieces (plus more for garnish)
Optional garnish: whipped cream and chocolate shavings

Chocolate Pots De Crème is an easy dessert that you can make at home. It's a rich, creamy, and decadent dessert that will be sure to impress your guests! All you need are a few simple ingredients: heavy cream, egg yolks, granulated white sugar, kosher salt, pure vanilla extract, and 6 oz. of bittersweet chocolate. Simply mix the ingredients together and place them in a dish before baking it in the oven until the dessert is set. You can garnish with whipped cream and chocolate shavings for an extra special touch! Enjoy this delicious dessert at your next gathering - your guests won't be able to resist it!
Happy baking!

Coconut Cookies

Ingredients
1/2 c. unsalted butter, melted
1/3 c. (70 g.) brown sugar
1/3 c. (70 g.) granulated sugar
1 large egg
1/2 tsp. pure vanilla extract
1 1/2 c. (180 g.) almond flour
1/2 tsp. baking soda
1/2 tsp. kosher salt
2 1/2 c. unsweetened coconut flakes, toasted, divided

Coconut cookies are a delicious dessert that can be easily made at home. With just the right combination of ingredients, you can create these tasty treats in no time. To make coconut cookies, melt 1/2 cup of unsalted butter and mix it with 1/3 cup of brown sugar and 1/3 cup of granulated sugar. Then add in 1 large egg and 1/2 teaspoon of pure vanilla extract. Next, mix together 1 1/2 cups of almond flour, 1/2 teaspoon of baking soda and 1/2 teaspoon of kosher salt. Finally, fold in 2 1/2 cups of toasted unsweetened coconut flakes and stir until the ingredients are combined. Bake the cookies in a preheated oven at 350F for 12-15 minutes until lightly browned. Enjoy your homemade coconut cookies as a dessert or snack! These deliciously easy dessert ideas are sure to be a hit with everyone.

As an added bonus, you can customize the cookie dough according to your taste. For example, add in some chopped nuts or chocolate chips for a tasty twist. You can also play around with different types of flours like oat flour or coconut flour if you'd like! Enjoy experimenting and have fun baking!

Coconut cookies are a great dessert to make at home and the perfect treat for any occasion. With just a few simple ingredients, you can quickly whip up a batch of delicious coconut cookies that your family and friends will love! Be sure to give these easy dessert ideas a try today!

Making dessert has never been easier with these yummy coconut cookies. With just a few ingredients and some time in the oven, you can create delicious treats that everyone will love! Enjoy experimenting with different variations to make these cookies your own! These easy dessert ideas are sure to be enjoyed by all. So get baking today and enjoy the deliciousness of homemade coconut cookies!

Profiteroles

Ingredients
FOR THE PÂTE À CHOUX
1 c. water
1/2 c. (1 stick) unsalted butter, cut into ½" cubes
Pinch kosher salt
1 1/4 c. all-purpose flour
4 to 5 large eggs
Ice cream, for serving
FOR THE CHOCOLATE SAUCE
1/2 c. heavy cream
1 1/2 c. semisweet chocolate chips
2 tbsp. coconut oil

Profiteroles are a classic dessert that can easily be made at home. Filled with ice cream and topped with chocolate sauce, they are the perfect indulgence!

To make profiteroles, start by making pâte à choux. Heat water, butter, and salt in a medium-sized saucepan until the butter melts. Remove from heat and add the flour, stirring until it forms a ball. Return to medium-high heat and stir for 1 minute or until the dough forms a thick paste that pulls away from the sides of the pan.

Transfer the dough to a large bowl and let cool for 5 minutes before adding 4 eggs one at a time, stirring until the dough comes together. Transfer to a piping bag and pipe small rounds onto parchment paper-lined baking sheets. Bake at 425°F for 15 minutes or until golden brown.

To make the chocolate sauce, heat cream in a small saucepan over medium-high heat until it comes to a simmer. Add the chocolate chips and coconut oil, stirring until the chocolate has melted. Let cool before serving with the profiteroles.

Profiteroles are a fun and easy dessert that can be enjoyed year-round! Whether you're hosting a dinner party or just looking for something to satisfy your sweet tooth, this classic dessert is sure to do the trick.
Enjoy!

Vanilla Milkshake

Ingredients
FOR THE ULTIMATE VANILLA MILKSHAKE
4 large scoops (about 1 1/2 c.) vanilla ice cream
1/4 c. milk
Whipped topping, for garnish
Sprinkles, for garnish
Maraschino cherry, for garnish

If you want a dessert that is easy to make, delicious and unique, then the ultimate Vanilla Milkshake is sure to be a hit. The ingredients for this milkshake are simple: four large scoops of vanilla ice cream, 1/4 cup of milk and some whipped topping, sprinkles and maraschino cherries for garnish.

To make the milkshake, simply add the ice cream and milk to a blender and blend until smooth. Pour into a tall glass or milkshake cup and top with whipped topping, sprinkles and a maraschino cherry. Enjoy this dessert in minutes!

For an even more decadent dessert experience, add a scoop of your favorite ice cream flavor for a swirled milkshake. Or top with chocolate syrup and even more sprinkles!

The ultimate Vanilla Milkshake is the perfect dessert idea to make at home. With just a few simple ingredients, you can have an amazing dessert that will have everyone asking for more.
Enjoy

Oreo Truffles

Ingredients
1 (14 oz.) package Oreos
8 oz. cream cheese, softened
1 tsp. pure vanilla extract
2 c. white chocolate chips, melted
2 tbsp. coconut oil
1/2 c. semisweet chocolate chips

Oreo Truffles are a delicious dessert that you can make at home with minimal effort. Perfect for any special occasion or just to satisfy your sweet tooth, these Oreo truffles will be sure to please everyone. All you need is 1 package of Oreos, 8oz of cream cheese, 1 teaspoon of pure vanilla extract, 2 cups of white chocolate chips, 2 tablespoons of coconut oil, and 1/2 cup of semi-sweet chocolate chips.

To make the Oreo truffle mixture, place all of the Oreos in a blender or food processor and blend until they form a fine crumb. In a bowl, mix together the cream cheese, vanilla extract, and Oreo crumbs until they are evenly combined. Roll the mixture into small balls and place on a baking sheet lined with parchment paper. Place the baking sheet in the freezer for at least an hour to let the truffles set up.

Once the truffles have set up, it's time to dip them in chocolate! Heat the white chocolate chips and coconut oil in a microwave-safe bowl for one minute, stirring every 15 seconds until melted. Place each truffle into the melted chocolate and use a spoon to coat them evenly. Place each coated truffle on a baking sheet lined with parchment paper and let them cool completely.

Once the truffles are cool, melt the semi-sweet chocolate chips in a microwave-safe bowl and use a spoon to drizzle it on top of each truffle. Place the baking sheet back in the freezer for 15 minutes to let the chocolate set up before serving.
Enjoy!

Pumpkin Cheesecake Roll

Ingredients

FOR THE CAKE
- Cooking spray
- 1 c. granulated sugar
- 3/4 c. all-purpose flour
- 1/2 tsp. kosher salt
- 1 tsp. baking soda
- 1/2 tsp. pumpkin spice
- 3 large eggs
- 2/3 c. pumpkin puree
- Powdered sugar, for rolling

FOR FILLING
- 12 oz. cream cheese, softened
- 1 tbsp. butter, melted
- 1 tsp. pure vanilla extract
- 1 1/4 c. powdered sugar
- 1/2 tsp. kosher salt

Have you been looking for dessert ideas that are easy to make at home? If so, why not try making a homemade Pumpkin Cheesecake Roll? It's a delicious dessert that looks impressive and is surprisingly easy to make. All you need are a few simple ingredients like cooking spray, granulated sugar, all-purpose flour, baking soda, pumpkin spice, eggs, pumpkin puree, cream cheese, butter, powdered sugar and salt. Start by preheating your oven to 350°F and lightly grease a 17x12-inch sheet pan with cooking spray. Next, in a large bowl whisk together the granulated sugar, flour, salt, baking soda and pumpkin spice. In a separate bowl beat together the eggs and pumpkin puree until smooth. Then add this mixture to the dry ingredients, stirring until just combined. Spread the batter evenly into the prepared pan and bake for about 15 minutes or until a toothpick inserted in the center comes out clean. Allow the cake to cool for five minutes before sprinkling it with powdered sugar and rolling it up. To make the filling, in a medium bowl beat together the cream cheese, butter, vanilla extract and powdered sugar until light and fluffy. Once the cake has cooled completely, unroll it carefully and spread the cream cheese mixture over top of it. Then roll it back up tightly and chill for at least two hours before serving.

Enjoy

Homemade Churros

Ingredients
FOR THE CHURROS
1 c. water
6 tbsp. butter
2 tbsp. granulated sugar
1 tsp. pure vanilla extract
1 c. all-purpose flour
1 tsp. kosher salt
2 large eggs
Vegetable oil, for frying
Cinnamon sugar
FOR THE CHOCOLATE DIPPING SAUCE
3/4 c. dark chocolate chips
3/4 c. heavy cream
1 tsp. ground cinnamon
1/4 tsp. kosher salt

Treat your family to a special sweet treat by making homemade churros! This Kid Friendly Dessert Recipe is easy to make and sure to be a hit. Start out by combining the water, butter, sugar, vanilla extract, flour and salt in a medium saucepan over medium-high heat. Stir until the mixture is smooth and comes together. Turn the heat to low, then add the eggs and mix until everything is combined. Heat a large pot of vegetable oil over high heat. Once it's hot enough, spoon the churro batter into the hot oil in batches, being careful not to overcrowd the pot. Fry for 3-4 minutes or until golden brown. Remove with a slotted spoon and transfer to a paper towel-lined plate. Sprinkle with cinnamon sugar while still warm. For the Chocolate Dipping Sauce: Combine the chocolate chips, cream, cinnamon, and salt in a medium saucepan over medium heat. Stir until the mixture is melted and combined. Serve churros with chocolate dipping sauce for a truly decadent dessert. Enjoy!

This Kid Friendly Dessert Recipe is sure to please the entire family and make your next gathering that much sweeter. Whether you're hosting a birthday party or just looking for an excuse to eat dessert, homemade churros with chocolate dipping sauce are always a hit. Get creative and top your churros with your favorite toppings for an extra special treat.
Enjoy!

Chocolate Pudding

Ingredients
1/2 c. granulated sugar
1/4 c. unsweetened cocoa powder
2 tbsp. cornstarch
1/2 tsp. kosher salt
2 1/2 c. milk
3 large egg yolks
3 oz. chopped bittersweet chocolate
2 tbsp. butter
1 tsp. pure vanilla extract
Whipped cream, for serving
Chocolate shavings, for serving

Chocolate Pudding is a classic, kid-friendly dessert that can be easily made with just a few ingredients. This recipe combines granulated sugar, unsweetened cocoa powder, cornstarch, salt, milk, egg yolks, bittersweet chocolate, butter and vanilla extract to create the perfect combination of creamy and rich. The result is a smooth and delicious pudding that will please everyone in the family. To serve, top with freshly whipped cream and chocolate shavings for an extra special treat. Kids will love this simple yet incredibly tasty dessert! With just a few ingredients, you can whip up this Kid Friendly Dessert Recipe in no time at all. So why not try this delicious Chocolate Pudding today? It's sure to be a hit with your family!
Enjoy!

Strawberry Shortcake Cookies

Ingredients
Cooking spray
3/4 c. chopped strawberries
1 tbsp. lemon juice
1/2 c. plus 1 tbsp. granulated sugar
2 c. all-purpose flour
1/2 tsp. baking powder
1/4 tsp. kosher salt
1/2 c. butter, softened
1/4 c. packed light brown sugar
1 large egg
1 tsp. pure vanilla extract
FOR THE FILLING
4 tbsp. cream cheese, softened
3 tbsp. powdered sugar
Zest of 1 lemon

Strawberry Shortcake Cookies are a fun and kid-friendly dessert recipe that can be made in no time. With just a few ingredients, you can create delicious cookies filled with sweet strawberries and lemon zest. Start by preheating your oven to 350°F then lightly spray two baking sheets with cooking spray. In a medium bowl, mix together the chopped strawberries, lemon juice and 1 tablespoon of granulated sugar. Set aside for about 10 minutes until the mixture thickens.

In a separate bowl, whisk together the flour, baking powder, salt and remaining granulated sugar. Cut in the butter with a pastry blender or two knives until the mixture resembles coarse crumbs. Then stir in the brown sugar.

In a small bowl, whisk together the egg and vanilla extract until combined. Add to the dry ingredients and mix until just combined. Press down the dough gently with your hands then divide into two portions. Roll each portion of dough out onto a lightly floured surface to about ¼ inch thickness. Cut out circles with a cookie cutter then place on the prepared baking sheets.

To make the filling, combine cream cheese, powdered sugar and lemon zest in a small bowl. Place 1 teaspoon of filling into the center of each cookie circle. Place second dough circles over the top and press down gently around the edges to seal. Bake for 8-10 minutes or until lightly golden. Let cool on the baking sheets for about 5 minutes before serving.
Enjoy!

Chess Pie

Ingredients
1 pie crust
4 large eggs
1 1/2 c. granulated sugar
1/2 c. (1 stick) butter, melted and cooled slightly
1/4 c. milk
1 tbsp. white vinegar
2 tsp. pure vanilla extract
1/4 c. cornmeal
1 tbsp. all-purpose flour
1/2 tsp. kosher salt

Chess Pie is a classic dessert recipe that's perfect for any occasion. Kid friendly and easy to make, this creamy and delicious pie is sure to be a hit with the whole family! To get started, you will need a 9-inch deep dish pie crust, 4 large eggs, 1 1/2 cups of granulated sugar, 1/2 cup of butter (1 stick), melted and cooled slightly, 1/4 cup of milk, 1 tablespoon of white vinegar, 2 teaspoons of pure vanilla extract, 1/4 cup of cornmeal, 1 tablespoon of all-purpose flour, and 1/2 teaspoon of kosher salt.

Begin by preheating the oven to 350 degrees F. Place the pie crust in a 9-inch deep dish pie pan and set aside. In a medium bowl, whisk together all of the ingredients until well combined. Pour the mixture into the prepared crust and bake for 45 minutes or until golden brown. Allow to cool slightly before serving and enjoy! Kid friendly and delicious, this Chess Pie recipe is sure to be a hit with the whole family.
Enjoy!

Coconut Macaroons

Ingredients
Cooking spray
3 large egg whites
2/3 c. granulated sugar
1/2 tsp. pure vanilla extract
Pinch kosher salt
5 c. sweetened shredded coconut
FOR CHOCOLATE MACAROONS
1/4 c. unsweetened cocoa powder
1 1/2 c. chocolate chips, melted, divided
1 tbsp. coconut oil

If you're looking for a kid-friendly dessert recipe, macaroons are the perfect choice! Macaroons are easy to make, require minimal ingredients, and can be customized to your family's tastes. To make plain macaroons, begin by preheating oven to 350 degrees Fahrenheit and lightly spraying two baking sheets with cooking spray. In a medium bowl, whisk together the egg whites, granulated sugar, vanilla extract, and salt until combined. Gently stir in 5 cups of shredded coconut until all ingredients are well blended. Using an ice cream scoop or spoon, drop heaping tablespoons of the mixture onto the prepared baking sheets, spacing each cookie about 2 inches apart. Bake for 12-15 minutes or until golden. Allow to cool before serving.

For a chocolate twist on the classic macaroon, begin by preheating oven and lightly spraying baking sheets with cooking spray as directed above. In a medium bowl, whisk together the egg whites, granulated sugar, vanilla extract, salt and cocoa powder until combined. Gently stir in 5 cups of shredded coconut until all ingredients are well blended. Melt 1 cup of chocolate chips and mix with 1 tablespoon of coconut oil. Drop heaping tablespoons of the cookie mixture onto the prepared baking sheets, spacing each cookie about 2 inches apart. Bake for 12-15 minutes or until golden. Once out of the oven, top each cookie with a teaspoon of the melted chocolate mixture. Allow to cool before serving.
Enjoy!

Red Velvet Cake

Ingredients
Cooking spray
1 c. (2 sticks) butter, softened
1 c. granulated sugar
2 large eggs
1 tsp. pure vanilla extract
2 c. all-purpose flour
1/3 c. Dutch-processed cocoa powder
1 tsp. baking soda
1 tsp. kosher salt
1 c. buttermilk
1 tbsp. distilled white vinegar
2 tbsp. red food coloring
FOR CREAM CHEESE FROSTING
2 (8-oz.) blocks cream cheese, softened
1/2 c. (1 stick) butter, softened
4 c. powdered sugar
1 tsp. pure vanilla extract
1/4 tsp. Pinch kosher salt

Red Velvet Cake is a classic and kid friendly dessert recipe. This decadent cake is moist, fluffy, and delicious with its signature red hue. It's easy to make at home with just a few simple ingredients.

You'll need 2 sticks of butter that are softened, 1 cup of granulated sugar, 2 large eggs, 1 teaspoon of pure vanilla extract, 2 cups of all-purpose flour, 1/3 cup of Dutch-processed cocoa powder, 1 teaspoon of baking soda, 1 teaspoon of kosher salt, 1 cup of buttermilk, 1 tablespoon of distilled white vinegar and 2 tablespoons of red food coloring.

Begin by preheating your oven to 350 degrees F. Grease a 9-inch round baking pan with cooking spray and set aside. In a large bowl, cream together the butter and sugar until light and fluffy. Add in the eggs one at a time, followed by the vanilla extract.

In another bowl, whisk together the flour, cocoa powder, baking soda, and salt. In a separate bowl, mix together the buttermilk and vinegar. Add the dry ingredients to the wet ingredients in two batches, alternating with the buttermilk mixture. Stir in the red food color until just combined.

Pour batter into prepared baking pan and bake for 40-45 minutes or until a toothpick inserted into the center comes out clean. Let cool for at least 30 minutes, then frost with cream cheese frosting.

For the Cream Cheese Frosting: In a medium bowl, mix together softened cream cheese and butter until light and fluffy. Add in the powdered sugar one cup at a time, followed by vanilla extract and pinch of salt. Mix until ingredients are fully incorporated. Spread over cooled Red Velvet Cake and enjoy!

Chocolate Brownies

Ingredients
1 1/4 c. all-purpose flour
1 tsp. kosher salt
1/4 c. unsweetened cocoa powder
2 c. chocolate chips, divided
1 c. (2 sticks) butter, cut into 1" pieces
1 1/2 c. granulated sugar
1/2 c. packed brown sugar
5 large eggs, at room temperature
2 tsp. pure vanilla extract

Chocolate brownies are a classic and kid-friendly dessert that can be made with just a few pantry staples. With ingredients like all-purpose flour, kosher salt, unsweetened cocoa powder, chocolate chips, butter, granulated sugar, brown sugar, eggs and pure vanilla extract - you can whip up these delicious treats in no time. Perfect for a last minute dessert, chocolate brownies are sure to be a hit with the whole family. For an even more delicious treat, try adding some of your favorite mix-ins like chopped nuts, dried fruit or mini marshmallows. Add a scoop of ice cream and you have the perfect dessert! Get creative and have fun making these classic, kid-friendly chocolate brownies.
Enjoy!

Banana Split Pops

Ingredients
4 bananas
8 popsicle sticks
1 1/4 c. chocolate chips
1 tbsp. coconut oil
1/2 c. rainbow nonpareil sprinkles
Whipped cream, for serving

If you're looking for a fun and easy kid-friendly dessert recipe, then look no further than these Banana Pops! These tasty popsicles are made with simple ingredients like bananas, chocolate chips, coconut oil, and rainbow nonpareil sprinkles. They're the perfect treat to make with your little ones – just be sure to help them with the sticks and melty chocolate. Serve up with some freshly whipped cream and a maraschino cherry on top for a delicious dessert that everyone will love.
Enjoy!

Strawberry Gelato

Ingredients
2 cups whole milk
2 tablespoons light corn syrup
1 tablespoon honey
3/4 cup sugar

When it comes to kid-friendly desserts, nothing quite beats a delicious homemade strawberry gelato. Made with just a few simple ingredients like whole milk, light corn syrup, honey and sugar, this treat is sure to be a hit with kids of all ages! To make the perfect strawberry gelato, simply combine the milk, corn syrup and honey in a small saucepan and heat over medium-high heat until the sugar has dissolved. Once the mixture comes to a boil, remove it from the heat and stir in the sugar. Place the pan in the fridge for two hours or overnight to allow it to cool completely. Once cooled, strain the mixture through a fine mesh sieve into an ice cream maker and process according to the manufacturer's instructions. When the gelato is finished, scoop it into individual serving dishes or cone cups and garnish with fresh strawberries. Enjoy!

I want to take a moment to express my heartfelt gratitude for your recent purchase of my recipe book. As a passionate food lover, nothing makes me happier than sharing my favorite recipes with others. Your decision to invest in my book not only supports my dream, but also shows your commitment to expanding your culinary horizons.

I sincerely hope that the recipes in the book will inspire you to try new things and add some excitement to your meals.

Thank you again for your support and for being a part of this journey with me. I hope my book will bring you many happy and delicious moments in the kitchen.

www.ingramcontent.com/pod-product-compliance
Lightning Source LLC
Chambersburg PA
CBHW041151110526
44590CB00027B/4196